*To Paulette —
In hopes you will
take some time to re-connect
to a peaceful and beautiful place
within your soul —
Joanne
2015*

Centered

Angie's Extreme Stress Menders

Volume 2

©2015 Angie Grace. All rights reserved.

Visit Angie's website
for special web exclusives for colorists.

www.AngieGrace.com

Made in the USA
Lexington, KY
02 November 2015